First published March 2026

The author acknowledges the traditional custodians of the lands on which this story unfolds and pays respect to Elders past and present.

## Acknowledgments

This book may carry my name on the cover, but it was never written by one voice alone.

First and always, to Bev.

Mum, this story exists because you lived it — not loudly, not for recognition, but because it was the life that needed living. You were never "just" anything.

Thank you for trusting me with your memories. Thank you for filling in the gaps when my own recollections were still just fragments of dust and dogs and long paddocks. Thank you for your honesty — even when it would have been easier to let the stories soften around the edges.

To my sister Kim — my first witness and lifelong co-traveller.

You were there for the pink pom-pom beanies, the cattle tracks, the bus, the Sunday dresses stitched from cricket whites, and the long search for Dad's camp smoke on the horizon. Your memory has been a compass for this story.

Thank you for your perspective, your corrections and for sharing the load of remembering.

To both of you — this isn't just my version. It's ours.

And to the life that shaped us — the long paddock, the stock routes, the stations, the towns that held us briefly and let us go — thank you for the lessons that never left.

## Foreword

People used to ask me where I grew up. It sounded like a simple question, but it never had a simple answer. Town names didn't really fit, and addresses meant very little when you didn't stay long enough for them to stick. So instead, I'd usually ask something back.

"Do you know what a drover is?"

Most of the time — nine out of ten — they didn't. So I'd tell them.

"Have you ever seen one of those old American westerns?" I'd ask. "Cattle strung out across open country, a man on horseback pushing them along, wagons trailing behind?"

Usually they'd nod.

"Well," I'd say, "it was just like that. Only Australian."

I'd start with the basics. A drover moved cattle or sheep from one place to another. But that never felt like enough. Droving wasn't just movement. It was a way of life built around weather, markets, distance, and reputation. It meant leaving more often than staying. It meant that "home" could be a wagon, a hut, a station kitchen, or a borrowed patch of ground.

Many Australians do know the title The Drover's Wife by Henry Lawson. In that story, the wife is alone in the bush while her husband is away. It's powerful and stark, and it captures isolation well. But being a drover's wife was more than waiting at a slab hut with a broom in hand and a snake under the floorboards. That was only one version of the story. In our family, the drover's wife didn't stay behind. She rode the road with him.

A drover's wife was not just a wife.

She was camp cook, bookkeeper, nurse, teacher, mechanic, negotiator, strategist, and steady centre of gravity. She raised children between jobs. She packed up without warning. She made temporary places feel like something solid. She held the shape of the family while the road pulled at its edges.

My father, Laurie, was a drover. A good one. His name travelled ahead of him when work needed doing. My mother, Bev, travelled with him. She didn't follow. She stood alongside. If he moved stock, she moved a household. If he read country, she read people. Between them, they built a life that rarely stopped long enough to gather dust.

When I explain that, people usually lean back and say, "Mate, you should write a book."

Well, this is that book.

We're going to call it fiction. Not because the people aren't real — they are — and not because the life wasn't lived. Many of the names are real. The places are real. The events happened. I've shifted time here and there, tightened some seasons, stretched others, because real life doesn't unfold in neat chapters. It loops, overlaps, and refuses to sit still.

If I'd written it exactly as it happened, the story might never have ended.

And that, I suppose, would have been fitting.

Timmy

# Contents

# CHAPTER ONE - The Butter Factory Girl

The house sat back from the dusty road, crouched low under a wide verandah that ran the full width of its weatherboard face. Sunlight slid over the corrugated-iron roof, the tin winking here and there where a summer storm had scoured it clean. The verandah posts, paint long gone to grey, leaned ever so slightly, as though tired from holding up so much shade. In summer, the verandah was the place where wet washing flapped in the breeze and children sprawled on the boards with schoolbooks, their bare legs sticking to the warm timber as they traced sums in pencil or read adventure stories with the smell of Mum's baking drifting out from the kitchen. A couple of dogs usually lay stretched in the shade, twitching in their sleep, while flies droned lazily around the enamel water jug kept cool in a damp tea towel. From the verandah you could watch the whole world of Merrigum pass by. Neighbours heading to the shop, the postie rattling past on his bike, and the slow roll of clouds promising either much-needed rain or another false hope.

At the back, the verandah had been half-closed in with timber and flywire to make a sleepout, a narrow, breezy room where summer nights were spent under mosquito nets, the sound of crickets slipping through the mesh. In winter, the flywire rattled in the wind and the frosty air nipped at toes that strayed beyond the blankets. On hot days, the flywire screen door slammed and sang on its spring, the rasp of its hinges as familiar as the bark of the dog on the woodheap. The screen door was a constant in family life, marking the comings and goings of the household with its sharp clap and creak. Kids dashed through it on their way to fetch water or chase a ball, and visitors would pause on the step, calling out before pushing it open. In the quiet of the afternoon, its sudden bang was enough to bring Mum's voice from the kitchen, a reminder to "mind that door!", though everyone knew it would slam again before the hour was out

Three small sleepouts stood in a row at the far end of the yard, their corrugated-iron roofs catching the late sun. They were usually rented out to railway workers, men who rose before dawn and came home bone-tired, their boots thumping on the path as they passed the kitchen window, but when Grandma moved in after a stroke, the railway men moved on and the whole family spread out into them. Bev earned her own sleepout for keeping her room spotless, a small kingdom of her own in the back garden where she could arrange her few treasures just so, a china dog from the show, a neatly folded stack of magazines, and a vase of fresh flowers when the season allowed. At night, she'd lie in bed listening to the muffled sounds of the house, the rustle of the wind through the pepper trees, and the distant hum of a train sliding through the darkness. It was a place where she could dream her own dreams, away from the chatter of her sisters and the busy heart of the main house.

Bev was the third oldest of six children, five girls in a row, with the youngest a boy. Mum was pregnant when Dad went away to war, so another baby arrived while he was gone. The children were so young when he left that, when he finally came home in 1945, they didn't recognise him. They were waiting near the big horse trough at the Merrigum bus stop when he stepped down from the bus, and they all bolted, scattering like startled chooks, hiding behind fence posts and sheds. They'd never seen him before, and the sight of a tall man in a soldier's uniform, smiling but strange, was enough to send them running. Mum called them back, her voice full of laughter and tears, but they peeked out only cautiously, inching closer as if he might disappear again. In time, they learned his smell, his voice, and the sound of his boots on the verandah boards, but that first meeting stayed with them, a reminder of how the war had taken more than just years; it had taken the shape of their family and made it new again.

Next door stood the butter factory where her father, Harold, worked as a butter maker. The factory was as much Bev's playground as his workplace. While other kids played in their yards, she was pushing cream cans along rollers, watching churns as high as the ceiling work their magic, and learning to wrap butter by hand. When the trucks rolled in with fresh cream, she and the other kids would help lift the lids so her Dad could taste each batch with his spatula, spitting it neatly into his testing jug. She loved the sweet, rich smell that hung in the air, mingling with the faint tang of the cool, damp rooms where the butter was stored. Sometimes Harold would wink and slip her a small pat of fresh butter, still soft and golden, to spread on a crust of bread. The steady clank and hum of the machinery became part of her childhood soundtrack, and she

3

knew every corner of the place, from the slippery tiled floors to the warm, steamy washroom where the churns were scrubbed clean at the end of the day.

Harold often brought home a big bucket of cream, and Mum would turn it into ice cream, beating it once halfway through freezing, then again after tea, before the family gathered for the treat. There was always enough for seconds, and sometimes she'd sneak an extra spoonful for herself when no one was looking. On special occasions, Mum would whip the cream into butter and bake scones, serving them warm with jam, the kitchen filling with the rich, comforting scent.

Harold's talents didn't end at the factory gates. He fished in the irrigation channels, bringing home bags of slippery, wriggling catch for Mum to gut and scale, a chore she never loved but did all the same. Bev was the only child he'd take with him; the others got restless, skimming stones, but she was content to sit quietly with a line in the water.

Two rainwater tanks flanked the back like sentries, their rust-streaked bellies catching the drip from the gutters. Beyond them, a windmill turned with a lazy creak, pumping from a bore for the garden and the small orchard behind the house. The air smelled of woodsmoke from the kitchen stove and the faint sweetness of fallen apples in the long grass. The orchard was a place of its own adventures, climbing trees to reach the ripest fruit, chasing each other through the rows, or sitting in the grass sharing bites of a just-picked peach, its juice running down their wrists. In spring, the trees were frothy with blossom, petals drifting like confetti across the yard. Come autumn, the ground was littered with windfalls, some destined for Mum's pies and others for the chooks. The orchard was a world apart, a place where time slowed, and the worries of the grown-up world, bills, weather, and work felt very far away.

On the mostly vacant Telecom block next door, Harold had laid out a sprawling vegetable patch. Wide beds of dark soil ran straight as a ploughed furrow, bordered by narrow walking paths. In summer, fat pumpkins sprawled between rows of silverbeet and cabbages, carrots and beetroot pushed feathery tops through the dirt, beans clambered up teepees, and tomato vines leaned heavy on their stakes. Sweetcorn rose in a green army at the far end, tassels whispering in the breeze, while marigolds bobbed at the borders in bright bursts of gold and orange, their scent said to keep pests at bay. Harold tended the patch like a second job, rising early to water before the heat set in, and working the soil with a steady patience that seemed to make things grow faster. Bev and her siblings were often sent out with baskets to gather whatever was ready, armfuls of silverbeet, tomatoes warm from the sun, beans that snapped crisply in the hand. It was hard work sometimes, but the reward was seeing the table piled high with food they'd helped to grow.

In winter, frost silvered the edges of cabbage leaves, onions stood like green spears, broccoli and cauliflower curled in tight white heads, and peas fattened in their pods along wire trellises. The soil was darker then, damp and rich, steaming faintly as Harold worked with his beanie pulled low. Bev often trailed behind him, pretending to help but mostly watching, occasionally being trusted to thin the carrot seedlings or pick peas straight from the vine to eat raw.

Inside, the floorboards sang under each step. The kitchen was the warm heart, a blackened Metters stove squatted in the corner, a kettle always on the boil, and the scent of fresh bread lingering in the air. In the front room, faded rugs softened the boards, and a cast-iron fireplace waited for the first cold night of autumn.

Out back, the dunny sat like an afterthought at the edge of the yard, beyond the chook run and woodpile. A low picket fence marked the front boundary, leaning like it was bowing to visitors, and geraniums blazed red against the pale boards. The chooks provided eggs for breakfast, their cackling a familiar soundtrack to the morning, and sometimes one would escape, sending the children scrambling to herd it back.

It wasn't much by city measure, but it was a house that held its own, stitched into the rhythms of butter-making, fishing, gardening, and family life, stubborn and enduring, like the people who called Merrigum home.

# CHAPTER TWO - Learning to Work

Bev's first steps into the working world came early. By Saturday mornings, while other kids slept in or kicked a football down the street, she was already dusting, sweeping, and polishing at a lady's house in town. Ten shillings for a morning's work, more than enough pocket money for those days, and she earned every penny. She quickly learned that cleaning wasn't just about scrubbing floors or dusting mantels; it was about taking pride in every little detail, noticing the way sunlight caught a streak on glass, or how a vase of fresh flowers could change the feel of a whole room.

The lady she worked for kept a tidy home, but there were always little jobs that needed doing, polishing silver cutlery until it gleamed, folding linen so crisply it looked like new, or beating rugs out in the backyard until clouds of dust drifted into the air. Bev found a quiet satisfaction in the work and, more importantly, in the independence that came with earning her own money.

Soon after, the same lady asked Bev's mother if Bev could babysit for them. It was the start of something new. She was still at school then, but she liked the feeling of being trusted to keep a child safe and content. Evenings were spent reading picture books aloud, keeping little hands away from breakables, and rocking a baby to sleep while the wireless murmured in the background. She became skilled at coaxing giggles from toddlers and calming tears before they turned into full-blown wails.

By the time she left school, barely fifteen, Bev had set her sights on a job that would take her beyond Merrigum's dusty streets. Her first position was as a nanny for the Gribbin family. The work was steady, and the family kind, but it came with responsibility well beyond her years. From there, she went to work for the Armitages. He was a doctor in Deniliquin, and she joined them while they awaited the birth of their child. When the baby arrived, the household moved back to Upper Ryans Creek near Benalla, and Bev went too.

At sixteen-and-a-half, she was in charge of the newborn's care. The baby slept in her room, only carried to its mother for feeding before Bev changed and settled it again. Nights were long, with feeds and nappy changes, but she took the trust placed in her seriously. She learned to move through the house quietly, shushing the creak of floorboards so the rest of the household could sleep.

She learned more than childcare. Mrs. Armitage loved to entertain, and Bev, watching from the kitchen doorway, absorbed the rhythms of cooking for guests. She learned to prepare dishes in stages so everything arrived at the table hot, how to lay out a table so it looked inviting, and how to move through a kitchen without fuss. She mastered light-as-air sponge cakes, golden roasts with crisp potatoes, and fresh salads arranged with care.

When that job ended, Bev moved on to the Ross family, Dudley Ross at Holbrook. Her older sister was working at Rossmore and helped Bev get the position. The property sprawled across wide paddocks, and Bev learned to ride a horse by sheer instinct, galloping across open ground, hanging on for dear life, knowing only that the animal's job was to get her there and back. Her first attempt at dismounting ended in a heap in the dust, but she laughed it off and got right back on.

At Ross's, her days were full. She cared for another baby in her room, tended to older children, pegged washing on long lines that snapped in the wind, and baked loaves of bread for school lunches. She sometimes joined the men in the paddocks, helping bring in sheep, or rode into town for supplies with a shopping list folded neatly in her pocket. In the evenings, she'd pore over the pages of the Weekly Times, circling job advertisements for nannies and stockmen. She daydreamed about faraway towns, wondering what it would be like to live and work there.

One ad caught her eye, a family in Jerilderie with a café and fish-and-chip shop, looking for a nanny. She wrote away for the job and got it. That weekend, she went home without saying a word to her mother about her plan. On Monday, she simply boarded the bus to Jerilderie, strong-minded, independent, and determined to shape her life her own way.

The work in Jerilderie was different. She cared for the family's children, but the hum of the cafe became part of her days. She sometimes helped in the shop, battering fish, wrapping hot parcels in butcher's paper, and calling orders over the clatter of pans. Fridays were the busiest, customers queued at the counter, the air thick with the scent of vinegar and fried potatoes. Bev loved the rhythm of it, the quick hands and quick words it demanded.

It was there she first met the drover. He came in for meals, a man with the road in his eyes and the smell of dust and sheep on his clothes. They spoke in snatches between orders, small talk about the weather, the state of the roads, the places he'd been. His stories were peppered with long days in the saddle, flooded creeks, and the quiet beauty of nights under the stars.

When she eventually left Jerilderie for another job, she carried with her more than wages and experience — she had a pen pal. Over the next year, letters passed between them, carrying tales from the road and hints of a different life. She also picked up short-term work whenever she could, picking fruit under a blazing summer sun, sweeping wool in a shearing shed, helping with lamb marking, and even scrubbing out water troughs for pocket money.

Each job, no matter how small, taught her something new, how to work hard without complaint, how to fit into any household or crew, and how to keep her eyes on what lay ahead.

Bev was learning to work, but she was also learning to dream and the world beyond Merrigum was calling.

# CHAPTER THREE - The Drover

The first sign of them was the sound, a low, shifting murmur of bleats and barking, carrying on the still afternoon air. Then came the dust, curling above the pepper trees at the edge of town. Moments later, the mob appeared, spilling down Merrigum's main street in a slow-moving tide of wool.

The dogs worked the edges with quick, darting precision, their ears flicking at each whistle from the drover meandering behind them. He was a lean figure in the saddle, his shirt sleeves rolled, hat brim low, moving with the easy sway of a man who'd spent more days on horseback than on his own two feet.

Merrigum watched him pass. Kids on pushbikes weaved ahead of the sheep until a sharp bark from a dog sent them scattering. Folks nodded from verandahs, and the drover tipped his hat in return.

From her family's yard, Bev leaned against the fence and watched the scene unfold, the kind of thing she'd seen before, yet somehow different today. When the mob drew level, the drover glanced her way. He didn't slow, but the look was enough to stir something deep in her memory.

That evening, when she came home from work, Mum was waiting by the kitchen door.

"There's some bloke been hanging around, asking after you," she said, her voice curious but not unkind.

Bev thought little of it until later, sitting on the front ramp as the day cooled. A shadow passed, and there he was — the man from the saddle, minus his horse, dust still on his boots.

"G'day… thought that might be you," he said with a grin that was almost a challenge.

She hesitated, searching her mind.

"You don't even know who I am, do ya?" he teased.

She shook her head.

"I'm the drover," he said simply, and in that moment the letters she'd been receiving for months, words carried across miles of open country, took on a face, a voice, a presence.

Laurie came to the porch, resting a boot on the step as they talked. His time was short; he had a mob of sheep on the road and would be moving out of town again soon. But the conversation, like his letters, was laced with the promise of a different life, one beyond Merrigum's boundaries, lived under the wide sky.

Bev was seventeen, engaged to one of the Drage brothers, a local stockman. Their wedding was only three weeks away, her sister set to marry Drage's brother in a double ceremony. The dress was half-sewn in her room, and her path seemed already mapped. But that night, the quiet streets and starlit sky made her choice clear.

She packed a small bundle, slipped from the house, and walked to where Laurie waited. Behind her, the town slept, unaware that its morning gossip was already in motion.

By sunrise, the drover and the girl were gone, and Merrigum was left buzzing with the scandal, Bev had run off with the man on the horse. Her parents were frantic at first, until someone spotted her on the road with Laurie and his mob of sheep. Her father was ropeable, not only had she eloped with a bloody drover, but they weren't even married. He didn't speak to Laurie for seven years. Bev was already gone, bound for the long paddock.

There were things from Laurie's past not yet untangled, but that was bush life too — knots that took time.

Life was rough and raw. They travelled in a one-horse wagon, like something out of an American Western, only the big spoked wheels had been replaced with car tyres. They followed the stock routes from Moree in New South Wales to Victoria, the Outback stretching endlessly in every direction. Bev cooked over open fires, washed clothes in kerosene tins, and pegged laundry in the windblown emptiness of the One Tree Plain.

There were twenty-two dogs and seven horses, the dogs split into day and night crews. The day dogs worked the mob under Laurie's short, sharp commands: "Git away back!", "Away to me!", "Hold up!", "Bark up!", "Push 'em up!", "That'll do!". The night dogs were pegged nose-to-nose to guard against strays and intruders.

Each morning after billy tea and cereal, Bev would break camp and move the wagon ahead of the mob to the next watering reserve, usually about four miles on. She'd set up camp, start lunch, boil clothes, prop up her homemade washing line from a steel pole carried under the wagon, the night dogs riding along beside it. Once Laurie and the sheep arrived, she'd peg out the night dogs and get the camp in order.

Weeks on the long paddock blurred together, sheep strung out like chewed rope, dogs working the flanks like they had a mortgage to pay, dust thick as blowflies, and the steady bleating rolling on behind Bev's wagon.

Sheep were a different game to cattle. They drifted if you didn't watch them, wandering like kids after a circus. Tiger and Peg kept them tucked in, snapping round the leaders when they fanned out. Bev knew the rhythm, whistle, bark, shuffle back into line.

Late one summer afternoon, Finley appeared on the horizon. You could smell it before you saw it, wheat dust from the silos, fresh bread from the bakery, beer spilt on old pub boards.

Coming into town, there's the low hum of the silos, tall concrete sentinels guarding the season's grain. The main street's wide, with weatherboard shopfronts and verandas deep enough to shade a whole mob. The pub's the heart of it, horses tied to the rail, a couple of utes out front, and the clink of schooners inside. Kids in short trousers pedal past on pushbikes, and the smell of fresh bread drifts from the bakery. Folks here know what it is to live off the land. They tip their hats, ask after the country up north, and sometimes slip you a meat pie or a bottle of milk. Out here, miles from the city, it's the same rhythm it's been for decades, wheat, sheep, cattle, and the long straight road ahead. They pushed the woollies into the edge-of-town yards, old timber rails leaning but holding. The mob settled quickly, dust turning to mud at the trough, dogs drinking first.

Bev was heavily pregnant by then, her back aching, hands swollen from the work. As they closed the yard gate she told Laurie, "I need to get to the hospital." He shook his head. "Not 'til we put the sheep away." Once the mob was settled, he loaded her into the wagon and drove her into town. The next day, he was back, baby in Bev's arms, both bundled in blankets, and they were on the road again.

Nights on the plain were soft. Magpies packed it in, galahs grumbled in the gums, and the hiss of the billy carried over the quiet breathing of the sheep. Out by the fire, dogs curled at their boots, Bev cradled her newborn, and the long road waited in the dark. For a night or two, Finley felt like the middle of everywhere.

By the time the sun began to lean towards midday, Bev was already thinking ahead to lunch. Out here, meals weren't just a break in the day, they were an anchor. She'd get the campfire going well before the mob stopped, letting the flames settle into hot coals so the food could be half-cooked before they moved on again.

Laurie always said the sheep needed a spell every couple of miles. It wasn't just for them, the dogs, tongues lolling and coats dusted with burrs, needed water, shade, and a feed. Bev saw to that, making sure their water tins were full and their bellies taken care of before she thought of herself.

12

She kept to her own kind of order. The spare water from a nearby hole meant she could wash every day, and she did. If she didn't, the pile would get out of hand. She set up her own washing line, driving steel posts into the ground until they stood firm. Clothes were never flung over a fence, not on her watch. She was fussy about it too: if she found a stray singlet at the bottom of the basket, she'd shift everything along so all the singlets hung together, as they should.

She mostly pushed ahead of the mob, setting up lunch camp so that when the sheep came through, the dogs were ready to turn them back. It was a rhythm that became second nature.

The children grew up in that rhythm too. Vicki was born in Kyabram, joining her sister Kim, who, as a toddler, was tied to the shaft of the wagon in a little harness so she couldn't wander off or tumble into an irrigation channel. It might raise eyebrows now, but back then it was simply practical.

Other drovers could always tell when Bev had been at a reserve before them, the ground was raked clean in a wide circle around the camp. She did it so the kids wouldn't get prickled with bindis and the dogs wouldn't cut their feet on stones.

There were days that stuck in her memory like burrs in a dog's coat. Near Deniliquin, the rain came in hard, drumming on the canvas until everything was soaked. Laurie, thinking himself clever, rigged the tent so Bev could hang nappies around the fire to dry. The result: every last one turned black with soot.

The postman, who passed once a week with mail and supplies for the stations, stopped at their camp that day. He had a delivery from the agent, bread and a few other essentials. Bev laughed about the nappies, shaking her head, and the postman, with the quiet kindness bush folk are known for, offered to take them into Deniliquin. The next day, he returned with them, clean, white, and neatly folded from the laundromat.

Out here, it was the little things that stayed with you. The smell of smoke on clean washing. The wet dog smell of tired kelpies under the wagon.

The way kindness could turn up unannounced, riding down the track on a mailman's buggy.

# CHAPTER FOUR - The Wagon

By the time Vicki was born, the one-horse wagon was no longer enough.

There had been a kind of balance before that. Bedding rolled tight. Tin trunks wedged against the sides. A cradle secured so it wouldn't tip when the wheels struck a rut. It was cramped, but it held.

Another baby shifted the weight of things.

More nappies drying from a line strung between wagon rails. More blankets. More small garments folded into corners. The narrow body of the wagon began to feel less like adventure and more like arithmetic.

So they moved to a two-horse wagon.

It wasn't grand. Just broader through the middle, steadier on rough ground, built to carry more without complaint. Laurie saw it as practicality. The mob was growing. The family was growing. The wagon had to follow suit.

Bev agreed — with one condition.

No matter how tightly it was packed, no matter how many boxes were tied on top or wedged along the sides, there had to be room underneath for the sewing machine.

It was a hand-cranked machine, solid cast iron, heavy enough to bruise you if you weren't careful shifting it. You turned the wheel with one hand, steady and patient, and fed the material through with the other, keeping the line straight as best you could. It folded down into its wooden case and travelled wrapped in canvas beneath the wagon, as protected as anything could be out there. Plenty of things were left behind when the load got too heavy. That sewing machine never was.

She made all the girls' clothes on it. Dresses cut down from flour sacks. Hems let out as legs lengthened. Shirts reshaped from whatever fabric came to hand. In the evenings, when the sheep settled and the dogs lay quiet, the steady rhythm of the wheel would carry through camp, as familiar as the crackle of the fire.

The road decided most things.

But what her children wore — that remained hers.

The two-horse wagon creaked forward under its new weight, settling into its longer stride as if it had always known this was coming.

A Lesson in Sheep

They were just breaking camp on the road to Deniliquin, the wagon creaking forward while Laurie eased the mob out onto the track. The morning was steady, dogs working close, sheep flowing the way they should.

Then a horn split the air.

The sheep jolted as one.

It only took a second for a mob to lose its nerve. One sharp, unnatural sound and the leaders would turn, the tail would follow, and all that slow, patient work would unravel.

Bev didn't hesitate. She tied off the wagon reins, stepped down, and cut straight through the edge of the mob towards the noise.

A brand-new Holden sat nose-first in wool, horn blaring, driver pale and flustered as sheep pressed around his tyres.

She stepped to the window.

"Oi. That'll do."

It wasn't loud. It wasn't angry. It was simply certain.

The horn stopped.

"You can sit there quiet," she said, "and let them move round you. Or you can keep that up and we'll be here till dark. Your choice."

The man looked from her to the dogs to the long stretch of sheep behind her and seemed to realise he had misjudged the situation entirely.

He nodded.

Bev held his gaze another moment, then stepped back into the mob. The dogs, already reading the shift in tension, pushed the leaders forward again. Within minutes the sheep were flowing around the Holden like water around a rock.

Later that night, by the fire, Laurie shook his head.

"Some blokes," he said, "don't understand sheep."

Bev shrugged. "Or dogs."

Because the truth was, without the dogs, none of it worked.

Out there, sheep were one thing. Cattle were another. But dogs — dogs were the difference between order and chaos.

And among them all, there was one that stood apart.

A Red Dog Called Blue

Droving meant distance, not miles, but horizons. Sheep and cattle were pushed across country that baked and cracked in summer, flooded and swallowed hoof and boot in winter, and stretched so far a man could forget what fences looked like. Out there, a dog could not be ornamental. He had to be clever enough to think for himself, hard enough to take a kick, and loyal enough to circle back when the dust swallowed everything whole.

There were no tidy kennels in the bush, no catalogues promising fine bloodlines. A drover bred what worked. If a dog held cattle steady in the heat, if he could travel all day without quitting, if he knew the whistle before it was finished, he was bred. Performance mattered. Papers did not.

The Australian Cattle Dog, Blue Heeler to some, Red Heeler to others, came from that need. Crossed and recrossed in rough stockyards and lonely homesteads, shaped by dust, distance, and necessity. They were bred for stamina, for heat that shimmered like glass, for the instinct to nip and dart and turn half-wild cattle with nothing but timing and nerve.

Bluey was one of them.

A Red Heeler, though no one ever bothered correcting the name. There's something about those dogs, they carry a joke in them, or maybe it's stubbornness, so even red-coated and copper-bright, he answered to Bluey all the same.

Laurie had bred him himself, watched him tumble about the yard as a pup, all oversized paws and bright, measuring eyes. By the time he was grown he seemed to know every whistle Laurie could shape, every hand signal cut through the air. He worked close and low, silent when he needed to be, quick as thought.

On the long afternoons when the sheep were settled and the sun hung white and heavy above the plain, Kim and Vicki would slip away laughing, weaving in and out of the mob. Their pink pom-pom beanies bobbed like startled galahs among the woolly backs. Bluey would glance at Laurie, waiting.

Laurie let them run a little. Let childhood have its stretch.

But when they drifted too far, when the bush began to thicken and the ground dipped towards scrub — he'd lift two fingers to his lips and whistle.

"Blue. Go on, get 'em. Way back, Blue."

And Bluey would be gone in a heartbeat.

He'd thread through sheep and dust, darting left and right, sometimes leaping clean over a startled ewe, circling the girls with sharp little barks until their laughter turned and flowed back towards camp. He never touched them. Just pressure, presence, instinct. A neat, tidy gather every time.

Most drovers kept a string of dogs and turned them over when their pace dulled or their teeth wore down. A working dog was an asset, and assets moved on before they became a burden.

But Bluey had never been just that.

It happened quick, the way bush trouble always does.

One moment the girls were laughing. The next Bluey bolted.

Not the smooth, measured run of a gather, this was frantic. Barking, growling, tearing through the grass in tight, desperate circles. Kim and Vicki stood frozen, confusion wide in their eyes as Bluey lunged and wheeled around them, driving them back harder than he ever had before.

"Blue!" Laurie shouted.

The dog didn't answer.

Laurie swung down from his horse, boots hitting dirt, striding towards the commotion. He whistled sharp and shrill. Called again. Yelled.

Bluey did not break.

Then it came, a flash of striped muscle in the grass.

A tiger snake rose, hood flared, body coiled tight as rope. Bluey lunged first.

The strike was so fast Laurie barely saw it. A snap. A yelp that tore straight through him.

Bluey jumped back, shaking his head, then lunged again, fury and instinct outweighing pain. The snake struck once more before slithering off towards the reserve fence and disappearing into the scrub.

The sheep shifted. The wind stilled.

Bluey staggered.

Laurie reached him in three strides, dropping to his knees. Two puncture marks were already swelling on Bluey's front leg. The dog's breath came hard and shallow, eyes still fixed on the bush where the snake had vanished.

"Good boy," Laurie muttered, though his voice broke. "You daft, brave fool."

They carried him back to camp. The girls were silent now, clinging to each other.

The night was long.

Bluey trembled, vomited, lay still as stone. His leg swelled grotesque and tight. Laurie sat beside him with a lantern and a damp cloth, speaking softly the whole time — stories, nonsense, apologies. Once or twice Bluey's tail thumped weakly, as if to say he was still there.

By morning, he was.

It took weeks before Bluey could stand steady. Longer before he could walk without pain. The swelling went down, but the damage stayed. The leg never straightened properly again.

He learned to move with a hitch in his stride, a permanent, stubborn limp.

Laurie tried him once, months later, on a small mob near the yards. Bluey ran three strides and faltered. Not from lack of heart — that was still fierce and shining — but from a body that no longer matched his will.

Laurie called him off.

That was the last day Bluey worked cattle.

He stayed close after that. Took up watch by the homestead instead. Followed the girls to the dam and back. Lay in the dust near the shearing shed, eyes half-closed but always listening. When Laurie rode out with the other dogs, Bluey would watch from the gate, tail low but steady.

Most working dogs were sold on or put down before age claimed them. That was the way of it. Hard lives ended clean.

But Bluey stayed.

He grew grey around the muzzle. His limp deepened. The fire in him softened into something gentler. The girls grew taller than his head. Seasons turned and turned again.

And when he finally lay down one cool evening beneath the old river red gum near the homestead and did not rise again, it was not from snake or kick or exhaustion.

It was simply time.

Bluey was the only working dog Laurie ever kept who died of old age.

They buried him where he could see the open paddock.

Even years later, when Laurie whistled without thinking, part of him still expected to see a red dog — called Blue — running low and fast across the dust.

A normal drove could take anywhere from a few weeks to a couple of months, depending on distance, weather, and the country in between.

The 1950s were often remembered for the floods — seasons when the Long Paddock disappeared under water and the track turned into a bog, sheep bogging, wagons sinking, and every mile a battle.

But by the end of that decade, the country swung the other way.

The Big Dry took hold.

By the early 1960s, wheat harvests across central New South Wales had dropped sharply. Dams dried back, creeks stopped running, and paddocks that once carried stock turned to dust. Sheep farmers began losing animals not to disease or misadventure, but to hunger and thirst.

It wasn't a good time to be on the land.

They had just delivered a herd of cattle to Newmarket and were making their way back when the stock and station agent caught up with them.

He didn't waste time with pleasantries.

He was looking for Laurie.

Laurie was good at his job — not just good, but bloody good. When stock needed moving, when things went wrong, when time was tight, his name was the one passed along first. He could read country the way other men read a newspaper. He knew when to push and when to ease off, how to hold a mob together when heat and distance tried to pull it apart.

That kind of reputation travelled fast.

And now someone needed exactly that.

There were five thousand sheep up near the Gunbar–Merriwagga country. They weren't going to market, and they weren't being shifted to greener pasture — there wasn't any. The job was simple in theory and hard in practice.

Keep them alive.

The plan was to take them south, working along the travelling stock routes, following what water remained — tanks, bores, the occasional creek if it hadn't run dry — and make for Hay, where the Murrumbidgee still flowed and stock could at least be held together.

It was the kind of job that could go wrong quickly.

Laurie took it.

For the trip they picked up a young stockman named Jack. He was green enough to still listen more than he talked, but not so green he couldn't sit a horse or hold a line. Keen, wiry, and watching everything Laurie did like it might be the difference between getting it right or getting it wrong.

Five thousand sheep meant counting mattered.

Every time they pushed the mob into a stock reserve, they counted them in. Every time they moved out again, they counted them out.

Laurie counted under his breath as they passed.

"One… two… three…"

At each hundred he'd call it.

"Hundred."

Bev would quietly take a match from the matchbox and slip it into her pocket.

By the end of it, the matches told their own story.

23

Fifty-three matches meant 5,300.

Add the thirty-two Laurie held in his head — 5,332.

"Sounds about right," he'd say, and that was that.

It was simple, and it worked.

Gus was the horse that pulled the wagon — carrying the tools, shoeing gear, and all the bits and pieces you couldn't do without. If a horse threw a shoe, you fixed it then and there. No waiting, no hoping it would hold. Out there, you handled things when they happened.

Gus plodded along steady behind the mob, whether anyone held the reins or not. He knew his job as well as any dog.

One hot, dry afternoon, as they were pushing the sheep into a reserve, Gus caught sight of the dam.

What was left of the water must have looked better than anything he'd seen in days.

He drifted down towards it, still hitched to the wagon, and stepped in to drink.

But when he turned to come back out, the edge gave way beneath him.

The wagon tipped.

Then followed.

Over she went.

Tools, iron, shoeing gear — everything scattered and splashed into the mud and water.

No one said much.

They just got on with it.

Jack had been using that wagon as his sleeping quarters, but that night he took his swag and made himself a hip-and-shoulder hole under a tree a little way from camp. After a day like that, sleep came easily.

It was just on first light when Laurie heard it.

A low voice.

Not loud — more like someone trying not to make a sound.

"Laurie…"

He looked up.

The sky was just starting to grey, the kind of light that makes everything look half-formed.

Again.

"Laaaurie…"

He turned towards Jack's swag.

Jack lay stiff as a board, eyes wide, staring straight up.

Laurie walked over, slow and easy.

Jack didn't move.

Didn't speak.

Just gave the smallest nod towards his chest.

Laurie knelt down and peeled back the edge of the swag.

There, curled tight across Jack's chest, was a red-belly black snake.

25

Thick through the middle.

About four foot long.

Alive. Still.

Waiting.

Laurie glanced at Jack, took in the fear sitting just under the surface, and gave the faintest hint of a smile.

Then, in one smooth movement, he reached down and grabbed the snake by the tail.

Up it came, twisting.

Laurie swung it once, twice, building the motion, then cracked it down hard like a stockwhip.

A sharp, clean crack.

The head flew clear.

The body dropped at his feet.

Laurie stood, dusted his hands, and looked down at Jack.

"C'mon," he said. "Dogs'll get a feed out of that."

They kept moving.

Day after day, mile after mile, following what water they could find, pushing the sheep when they had to, holding them when they needed it. The country stayed hard. Dust hung in the air. Sheep fell behind and had to be lifted, coaxed, or left.

But they kept most of them alive.

By the time they worked their way back towards Jerilderie, they'd been on the road for over nine months.

That's when the word came through.

The drought had broken.

Rain had fallen back up north.

The station country was starting to come back.

There was no need to keep pushing on.

The owner had made arrangements.

The sheep would be trucked back from Jerilderie.

For the first time in months, the road didn't stretch endlessly ahead of them.

This time, it simply brought them in.

*Camped on the Stock Route*

*Everything travelled in the Wagon*

*And sometimes it didn't.*

*Red dog called Blue*

*Raised on the road -tethered to the wagon*

*When the road paused.*

*When the road was changing.*

*Crossing the new Hay Bridge*

*Published on the front page and courtesy of the Riverine Grazier*

*Friday, 22nd June, 1973*

*The Drover*

*The Wife*

*Bev and Stormy*

# CHAPTER FIVE - Station Life

Drovers like Laurie rarely spent all their time on the road. In between droving jobs, they worked on stations, cattle, sheep — it didn't matter, because that was how you stayed viable, visible, and fed. Droving was seasonal and irregular, mobs moved when markets shifted, when seasons broke, or when stations needed stock cleared, and no drover could afford to sit idle waiting for the next call.

Station work filled the gaps. It provided steady income, a roof, and feed for the family, and it kept a man's skills sharp. On a station, a drover was valued for his experience: reading country, handling stock quietly, fixing problems before they grew expensive. Managers knew that a good drover could step into almost any role, mustering, fencing, yard work, breaking horses, and do it without supervision.

Just as importantly, station work kept a drover connected. Word travelled fast in the bush, and reputation mattered. That was why they stayed on stations between droves, not drifting and not settling, but being known, being trusted, and keeping one foot already angled towards the next long push of cattle across open country.

For men like Laurie, it was neither drifting nor settling. It was a way of staying in motion even when the road was quiet, earning, waiting, and keeping one foot already pointed towards the next long push of cattle across open country.

Station life required a particular discipline, the ability to make the temporary feel permanent without ever believing it truly was. Bev learned that skill early. Properties came with houses or huts, sometimes nothing more than permission to park, but they offered something essential: a place to land while work held. Laurie followed the contracts where they appeared, and Bev followed with quiet calculation, weighing children, seasons, and effort. Sometimes they chose to stay. Often the choice was made for them.

That was how they ended up at Yanco Station.

Yanco Station felt different from the beginning. The land opened out instead of closing in, the paddocks rolling gently rather than pressing hard against the horizon. The homestead was weathered but solid, carrying the sense of a place that expected people to stay long enough to matter. The work was steady, and the days fell into patterns that didn't immediately threaten to break. For the first time in a long while, Bev felt herself slowing, not stopping, but easing into the idea that this might be a place they could hold for a bit.

Yanco was big country, and fence riding there wasn't a job you finished and came home from at night. It meant leaving camp before sunrise and not returning for days, sometimes weeks, following the boundary as it wound through scrub, gullies, and long open stretches where the silence pressed in as hard as the heat. He carried water, wire, tools, and what he needed on the saddle, trusting the horse beneath him and the country ahead.

On properties this size, the work had to be shared. A relief rider would cut straight across the station to a pre-arranged meeting point somewhere out on the boundary, riding through country rather than following the fence itself. When they met, horses were swapped, a few words exchanged, and Laurie would turn back towards camp while the other man took over the line. Sometimes that exchange happened six or eight times before the entire boundary was checked. More than once, the last rider hadn't even made it back in before Laurie was already heading out again, setting off for the next section as if the work folded endlessly in on itself.

Fence riding was slow, deliberate work. Every mile mattered. Every post and strand had to be seen. If something was missed, stock would find it long before a man ever did. By the time Laurie came back in, sunburned, dust-coated, quiet, he knew the land intimately: where water held, where fences failed after rain, where cattle tested their luck. That kind of knowledge made him useful. It also made him known.

While Laurie worked the edges of the property, Bev held its centre. With shearers and jackeroos on Yanco, she was once again taken on as the cook, rising before light to fire the stove and bake bread, feeding men who worked hard and ate harder. Meals ran on routine and expectation; there was no room for lateness or complaint. Bev ran the kitchen the way she ran everything else, steadily, efficiently, without noise. It anchored her days while Laurie was gone, giving shape to the long absences.

Years later, when that life was behind her and she went looking for work at the local hospital, the nurses had their own nurse's canteen, and they were looking for a cook. The head of the main kitchen asked "can you cook", Bev replied *"well I've cooked for shearers and jackeroos"*. He looked at her for a moment, then laughed and said, *"Well if you've cooked for those bastards, you can start tomorrow"*. Bev didn't smile. She didn't need to. She already knew exactly what she could do.

Because the stay stretched on, Bev unpacked more than she usually allowed herself to. Curtains went up properly. The wagon was parked as if it might not need to move again next week. She found a patch of ground that caught the sun and broke easily under the spade, and for once, she let herself imagine time differently.

The Garden

She planted vegetables.

Not just a token row, but a small patch, cabbage, silverbeet, carrots, the kind of things that took patience. Each morning she checked the soil, watered carefully, watched green push through brown. It wasn't just food. It was possibility. School terms instead of weeks. Seasons instead of jobs. She didn't say it aloud, but the thought settled all the same: maybe this is where we stay for a while.

Laurie took stock of the garden before he said anything else.

He stood there quietly, hat pushed back, looking at the neat rows Bev had coaxed out of borrowed earth. When he spoke, his voice was calm, already decided.

"We're moving on."

It wasn't an argument. It was information.

Something in Bev snapped— not loudly, not theatrically, but with a clean, final edge. She walked past him without a word, went straight to the patch, and began pulling. Carrots tore free from the ground, soil flying with them. Cabbage heads followed, heavy and hard in her hands. She turned and threw them at him, not wildly, not blindly, but with purpose. Vegetables struck his boots, his legs, thudded against his chest, burst apart in the dirt. Each one was an answer. Each one said what she wasn't going to waste breath on.

Laurie didn't move. He didn't step back. He just stood there and took it, until the patch was bare and her hands were empty. Laurie didn't stop her. He didn't apologise either. He waited until the patch was bare again, until the ground looked as it always did when they left, disturbed, but empty.

That night, Bev packed with the same efficiency she always did. By morning, Yanco Station looked as though they had only ever passed through.

But something stayed with her. Not the anger, that faded, but the knowledge of how close she had come to believing in permanence again. From then on, she planted carefully. Just enough to live on. Never enough to grieve.

Yanco taught her that lesson well: how to live as if you might stay, and how to leave without breaking.

She stopped planting deeply after that. But she never stopped keeping Sundays.

43

When Kim and Vicki were little, and they happened to be passing through a town big enough to have an Op Shop, Bev would make a quiet detour. She'd head straight to the rack of men's trousers and run her hand over the white cotton of cricket pants, checking the fabric between finger and thumb. If the cloth was still sound, she'd buy them.

Back at camp she'd sit with her sewing tin open beside her and pick the stitching out carefully, easing the seams apart until the fabric lay flat again. From those trousers she cut little white dresses. Nothing fancy. Just clean lines and a bit of swing in the skirt. Enough for Sunday.

If they were close to a town with a church, the girls wore those dresses to Sunday school, boots scrubbed, hair brushed, faces solemn in that way children get when they know something matters.

If there wasn't a church nearby, she dressed them anyway.

Sunday morning meant clean clothes, even if the congregation was sheep and galahs. She'd wash their faces, tie their ribbons, button the backs of those dresses stitched from second-hand cricket whites, and then they'd go for a walk across whatever paddock or roadside reserve they were camped beside.

It wasn't about being seen. It was about keeping shape in a life that could easily lose it.

The ironing was its own discipline.

She used a cast iron clothes iron, heavy and blunt, sitting it on a grate over the open fire to heat. There was no dial, no safety. She'd test it with a damp fingertip, listening for the hiss. Too cool and the creases wouldn't hold. Too hot and it would scorch straight through. She learned the timing the same way she learned everything else on the road — by feel.

She thought it was a real step up when Laurie brought home a kerosene-powered iron.

He'd found it somewhere along the track, second-hand but working. The little tank sat on top, flame steady inside, heating the plate evenly without guesswork. Bev turned it over in her hands, pretending to inspect it, though she was already pleased. It meant one less thing balanced over coals. One less small fight with the day.

The road still moved. Jobs still ended. Camps still packed down by morning. But on Sundays, the girls stood straight in white dresses pressed smooth by kerosene flame, and for a few hours, there was order.

She had learned not to plant too much into the ground.

But she still planted something into her children.

## CHAPTER SIX - Hay, Hell and Booligal

Long before the bridge was new and the trucks came through heavy with
sheep and other livestock, Banjo Paterson had already given Hay its
reputation. He wrote it into legend as a place where the heat pressed
down like a hand on the back of your neck, where dust worked its way
into your mouth and eyes and thoughts, and where the sun ruled without
mercy. In Hay Hell and Booligal, Hay was less a town than a trial, an
ordeal to be endured rather than passed through. Men wilted, horses
drooped, tempers flared, and the land itself seemed to conspire against
anyone foolish enough to linger. It was a country of mirages and
monotony, where distance stretched and shimmered, and the horizon
never quite came closer.

But Hay was more than a legend; it was a crossing point. Sitting squarely
on one of the main stock routes, it drew them back time and again,
drovers, families, mobs of sheep moving slowly under a sun that showed
no favour. Bev and Laurie passed through Hay not once but many times
over the years, its streets and paddocks becoming familiar in a way that
only repeated hardship allows. Sometimes they came with purpose,
paperwork, supplies, other times simply because the route demanded it.
Hay marked their journeys the way a gate marks a fence line:
unavoidable, unmistakable, and always remembered.

By the 1970s the town had changed, at least on the surface. There was a
new bridge now, concrete and confidence spanning the Murrumbidgee,
and people said progress had arrived. But the heat still came the same
way, the plains still rolled on without apology, and the rhythm of sheep
and dust and waiting still set the pace of life. Hay might have softened
around the edges, but it hadn't forgotten who it was. And anyone passing
through, drover, wife, children, sheep or cattle, soon learned that Hay
was still Hay, no matter what Banjo had called it, and no matter how
many years had gone by.

The One Tree Plain

They came in from the One Tree Plain, that long, flat nothing that shimmered under the sky like it had no intention of ever ending. It wasn't really a plain so much as a test of patience, mile after mile of open country with just the one lonely tree standing there, crooked and stubborn, as if it had decided to stay when everything else had moved on.

By the time the sheep reached the outskirts of Hay, Bev was already at the head of the mob, pregnant and steady on her feet, moving the way she always did, calm, certain, unreadable.

Bev had gone ahead earlier and hung the washing out. She'd laughed to herself as she pegged it, white shirts and little dresses snapping in the breeze, because out there on the One Tree Plain there was nothing else to see. Just the sheep and the sky and her washing flapping like a flag.

A fellow coming along the road had stopped at Laurie, squinting past the mob.

"Look mate," he'd said, scratching his head, "I'm not drunk, but is that washing flapping on the One Tree Plain?"

That was all it was.

As Hay came into view, Bev felt that familiar tightening in her chest, the way memory sometimes arrived without warning. She had to laugh to herself, remembering the last time they came through.

The Bridge and Mrs McGreggor

Back then it had been the old Hay bridge, with the hump in it. A nightmare for big mobs. Sheep didn't like the rise, didn't trust what they couldn't see on the other side. Many a drover had come unstuck there.

And then there was Mrs McGreggor.

Mrs McGreggor had a cleft palate and a hair lip, which made her talk kinda funny to some people, though no one ever laughed twice. She had three pet sheep, Billy, Daisy, and Nellie, and she charged drovers a small fee for her and her sheep's service.

She'd leave her sheep with the mob, walk over the bridge, then turn and call them. Billy, Daisy, and Nellie would trot up onto the bridge without hesitation, and the mob, trusting their own, would follow. Just like that, across the bridge and straight into Lachlan Street.

On this particular day, there was a young bloke trying to get over the bridge, but he had no idea what to do. As the sheep got closer, he would toot his horn, sending them scattering back the way they'd come.

Mrs McGreggor would call her sheep.

The sheep would come.

The horn would toot.

The sheep would scatter.

Again and again and again.

Finally, frustrated as all heck, Mrs McGreggor walked up the bridge and around to the front of the car. She put one foot up on the bumper, leaned in, stared straight into the young man's eyes with a scowl that made his blood curdle, and said,

"Go ahead, toot that horn one more time and you just see what happens."

The young bloke wound down his window. Through a lisp caused from the same affliction as Mrs McGreggor's, though hidden by a youthful, full moustache, he said,

"What's the matter, missus?" he asked, his s's slipping into th's.

Mrs McGreggor's jaw dropped. She turned red with rage.

"Mock me, will ya, ya bastard,"

She snapped, leaning in so close he could count the freckles on her nose. "You toot that horn one more time and I'll shove it so far up your backside you'll be bleatin' with the rest of 'em."

That did it.

The young bloke went pale, eyes wide, moustache twitching. Without another word he slammed the car into reverse and backed, slowly, carefully, humiliatingly, back over the bridge, sheep, Billy, Daisy and Nellie watching the whole thing like a jury that had already reached a verdict.

Mrs McGreggor dusted off her hands, called her sheep, and led the mob across as neat as you please.

Later that afternoon, the same young bloke wandered into the pub, trying to look like nothing in the world had rattled him. He ordered a beer, took a long pull, and was just about halfway through when the door opened.

In walked Mrs McGreggor.

He froze.

The glass hovered mid-air. His eyes bulged. Colour drained from his face so fast you'd think someone had pulled a plug. Without even putting the beer down, he spun on his heel, bolted for the door, and was out the pub and halfway down the street before Mrs McGreggor had even spotted him.

She ordered herself a lemonade, leaned on the bar, and smiled to herself.

Billy, Daisy and Nellie would've been proud.

Bev smiled at the memory as the sheep flowed forward now, easy as water. This time there was no hump to worry about. The new Hay bridge stood wide and flat, waiting.

People lined the street. It wasn't every day a mob like this came through anymore, not since things had started changing. Not since trucks and rail and fenced paddocks. This was the first mob of sheep to cross the new bridge, and the town knew it. It was such an event it made the front page of the local paper the next day.

Not long before they passed through Hay that time, Laurie finally tied off a loose end he'd carried for years. He tracked his first wife down to Fairlea Women's Prison and went there with the papers folded in his pocket. The visit was brief and awkward, stripped of anything that might have once mattered. When he explained why he was there, the matron looked at him for a long moment and said, flatly, "bloody drovers, drovers and shearers…". Papers were signed. A door closed. Something old and unfinished was finally put down. It wasn't about the past anymore — it was about clearing the road ahead. Laurie came back knowing there was nothing left in the way now. They could marry. They could stop explaining themselves.


Born in Hay

Then Shane decided to arrive. The road stretched long and flat ahead of them, heat shimmering off the bitumen, the country giving no sign that anything out of the ordinary was about to happen. Bev later remembered only in fragments, the hospital room, the clipped urgency in unfamiliar voices, the sense that time had narrowed to something fragile and exact.

Shane came fast, and wrong. The umbilical cord was wrapped around his throat, tight enough to turn him blue, tight enough to steal his first cry. For a moment, everything stopped. Then hands were working, voices sharpened, the room filled with motion and breath and command. Someone acted quickly enough. Someone knew what to do. And then, just as suddenly, Shane cried. Colour returned. Life resumed its hold.

Bev held him afterward without shaking or tears, simply registering the weight of him, the fact of him. By then she understood how narrow the margin could be. Survival wasn't guaranteed by toughness alone. Sometimes it was timing. Sometimes it was luck.

Years later, Shane would tell people, half joking, half serious, that he and Jesus had something in common. Both born in Hay. It became one of his stories, delivered with a grin, but beneath it sat something truer: an early sense that he had arrived by chance, that staying was never quite assured.

At the time, there was no space to dwell on it. Life resumed its forward pull. They returned to work, to borrowed ground, to a way of living that never paused long enough for reflection.

For a time, the wagon was enough. Everything they owned had to justify itself. Space was rationed, routines refined, corners reused until nothing went to waste. Bev knew how to live small without feeling diminished. But as the family grew, the limits of canvas and timber grew sharper too. Babies needed warmth and privacy. Children needed room. Dignity began to matter in ways it hadn't before.

The Bus

After Shane arrived, the wagon was no longer enough.

That was when the bus came. Old, stripped, unwanted by anyone else, but solid. Laurie saw structure where others saw scrap. Bev saw walls that stayed put. Together they pulled out seats, built bunks, claimed corners for storage and cooking. It wasn't pretty, but it was theirs. It could hold them all.

The wagon wasn't abandoned. It followed behind, lighter now, storage and memory more than home.

When the stock and station agent came by, he didn't interrupt. He watched for a while, the children underfoot, the tools scattered, the bus half-open to the sky. Eventually he nodded, said it looked "about right." Bev turned to Laurie then and said, *"I'm not bloody going anywhere."* But even as the words left her mouth, she knew better. She knew how this life worked — the road, the work, and whatever it took to keep them moving.

By now, she'd been driving the bus long enough to know it like she knew the road. The day before, she'd gone into Hay because they needed another permit for the sheep to cross the bridge. Laurie stayed back with the mob, but before she left she said, half offhand, "Maybe I should get my license while I'm there."

Laurie laughed. "You don't even know the questions."

So she took the bus into town anyway, kids rattling around behind her, dust and wool still clinging to everything like it always did. She got the permit sorted, no fuss, then turned back to the cop behind the counter.

"While I'm here," Bev said, "I might get my license."

The cop leaned back in his chair and looked at her over the top of his glasses.

"Can you drive?" he asked.

"Yes."

"What d'you drive?"

"That." She nodded towards the window, where the bus sat baking in the sun.

Truth was, the cop had been watching her drive that bloody thing for the past five months, in and out of town for supplies, permits, odds and ends. He'd seen her hop down with a kid on her hip, reverse that bus into spots men twice her size wouldn't even attempt, swing it around corners like it was nothing.

He didn't ask another question. Didn't pull out a test or a form. Just nodded, reached for the book, filled it in, and slid it across the counter.

"There you go," he said.

And that was that.

She walked back out into Lachlan Street with it folded in her pocket, kid on her hip, the bus waiting where she'd left it, Kim's pony tied up behind the driver's seat like always, Vicki asleep on the bunk, and another day of the road stretching out ahead of them.

The Horse Float

Once Bev had her licence, the bus became more than just transport. It was the centre of everything — the kids, the dogs, supplies, and whatever else needed shifting from one place to the next.

Kim's pony, Wee Jenny — a little Welshie mare — travelled inside the bus behind the driver's seat, tied where she could ride steady while the road rolled past.

Laurie, of course, was never one to leave things alone for long.

Before long he'd started building something else to tow behind it.

Not every horse was built for the long paddock.

Drovers' horses were tough creatures, lean and hard from years of travelling. They could walk day after day beside a mob, living off rough grass and whatever waterholes turned up along the route. But the horse Laurie had been asked to collect this time wasn't one of those.

It belonged to a bloke down south who needed it delivered home, and Laurie, already moving a mob through that country, had agreed to do the favour.

The horse was a riding horse, well looked after and not used to travelling miles behind sheep. If they'd pushed it along the stock route it would have arrived looking like a hat rack.

Laurie reckoned there was a better way.

So he built a float.

Not the sort you see behind utes these days. This was bush engineering. Laurie found an old trailer frame, welded up a set of rails high enough to keep a horse steady, and laid planks across the floor. A simple ramp went on the back and a rail across the front so the horse couldn't lunge forward when the road dipped.

It wasn't pretty, but it was solid.

The idea was simple enough. Instead of walking the horse for miles behind the mob, they could load it on the float and tow it behind the bus so it wouldn't lose too much condition on the journey.

Laurie stood back when he finished it, hands on his hips, studying his handiwork.

"That'll do," he said.

The horse loaded well enough. Nervous at first, stamping and snorting as horses do when they're asked to trust something unfamiliar, but once it settled it stood quietly inside the rails.

Of course, Laurie wasn't the one driving.

Bev was.

That meant every day ran the same way it always did. In the mornings she'd head off ahead of the mob in the bus to set up the next camp. Now she had the float rattling along behind her as well.

At every stop she had another job to do.

She'd drop the ramp, lead the horse down so it could stretch its legs and graze while the mob and dogs came through, then load it up again when it was time to move on.

Driving the bus was one thing. She'd been doing that long enough. But towing a horse float was something else entirely. Every bump tugged at the back of the bus and every corner had to be taken wider than usual.

Laurie rode behind with the sheep like none of it concerned him.

Inside the bus, Wee Jenny stood tied behind the driver's seat as she always did, calm as anything while the road rolled away beneath them.

Bev kept the speed steady and her hands firm on the wheel, glancing in the mirror now and then.

The horse rode quietly most of the way, stepping down at each camp to graze before climbing back up the ramp again when it was time to move on.

By the time they got close to the horse's new home, it still looked fresh enough to make a good impression.

Laurie grinned when they unloaded it for the last time.

"Worked alright," he said.

Bev climbed down stiffly from the bus and looked back at the float.

"Next time," she said dryly, "you can bloody drive it."

Laurie just laughed.

# CHAPTER SEVEN - Merrigum

Bev made a point of getting back to Merrigum whenever she could.

It wasn't easy. The road never ran straight between jobs, and money didn't stretch just because you wanted it to. But if there was a gap between droves, or a station job that ended within striking distance, she'd load the kids up and head home.

Home wasn't really home anymore — not the way it once had been — but it was where Nan and Pop were. And no matter how far she'd gone or what choices she'd made, she wasn't about to let her children grow up not knowing their grandparents.

The kids always burst in first.

Through the front gate, around the back of the house and straight through the wire screen door that slapped shut behind them and sang on its spring.

Nan was at the wood stove, as she always was, back slightly bent, apron dusted with flour. The kettle rattled gently on the iron plate. The kitchen smelt of onions, tomato sauce, and woodsmoke — a smell Bev could have found blindfolded.

Pop sat at the long kitchen table, solid and square as ever, sleeves rolled, forearms thick and browned from a lifetime of work. Robert sat up the other end, lanky and loose-limbed, halfway through a bowl of spaghetti bolognese.

The kids ran straight to Nan.

There were kisses, hands on cheeks, loud greetings, overlapping chatter.

Bev followed, smiling despite herself. Laurie came in last, ducking slightly under the doorframe, dust still clinging to his boots.

"G'day, Pop," he said, same as he always did.

And just like all the times before it, Harold did not answer.

Not a grunt. Not a nod. Not even the smallest flick of acknowledgement.

It wasn't loud hostility. It was worse than that. It was deliberate absence.

The first few times it had happened, Bev had let it pass. She'd told herself time would fix it. That Pop would come round. That stubbornness ran in the blood and needed to burn itself out.

Seven years is a long time to burn.

Laurie stood there a moment longer than necessary, then moved to the bench, as if nothing had happened. As if he were invisible.

The kids didn't notice. They were too busy telling Nan about dogs and sheep and camps and rivers. Robert kept eating, eyes fixed firmly on his plate.

Bev watched her father.

The lines around his mouth. The set of his jaw. The way he held himself like the room belonged to him.

She thought about the wagon. The long paddock. The snake bites and late nights. The babies born and raised without complaint. The life she had chosen.

She thought about her children.

And something in her shifted.

Spaghetti on Top

She stepped forward.

"Dad."

No answer.

"Dad."

He looked up at her then, slow and heavy, but still said nothing.

The room quietened, just slightly.

"You need to accept Laurie and I are together," she said, steady as a fence post. "He's the father of your grandkids."

Silence.

"If you can't be civil to him," she continued, voice low and clear, "then I'll piss off with the kids. And you won't see us again."

Nan kept stirring at the stove, stone deaf to it all.

Robert's fork hovered mid-air.

Pop stared at her, stunned less by the words than by the fact she'd spoken them.

Bev didn't blink.

She reached across the table.

His bowl of spaghetti bolognese was still half full, steam rising off it.

Before anyone could quite process what was happening, she picked it up and turned it over — neatly, decisively — onto her father's head.

The bowl landed with a dull ceramic thud.

For a moment, no one moved.

Spaghetti slid slowly down Harold's face. Tomato sauce tracked along the lines of his cheeks and dripped from the end of his nose onto his shirtfront.

He sat there, rigid, blinking through mince and pasta.

Nan turned from the stove, wiping her hands on her apron.

"Sit yourselves down," she said brightly, as though nothing unusual was happening at all.

Robert stared at his father, then at the empty place at the table where his father's bowl had once been, then back at his father, then back to his own plate, and very deliberately resumed eating what was left on it.

Laurie didn't move.

Bev stood straight, breathing hard but not shaking.

No one laughed.

It wasn't funny.

It was final.

Pop lifted the bowl off his head slowly and set it down on the table. Sauce dripped onto the table cloth.

He looked at Laurie.

Really looked at him.

For the first time in years.

A long, measuring silence.

Then he grunted.

It wasn't an apology.

It wasn't affection.

But it was acknowledgement.

Laurie nodded once.

That was all.

After the spaghetti, things changed.

Not in a dramatic way. No embraces. No long speeches. But Harold began answering Laurie when he spoke. Cups of tea were poured without hesitation. Questions were asked about stock, about roads, about weather. Civil. Measured. Enough.

It made a difference.

The Dodge Run

Timmy was probably the first birth where there was something resembling a plan.

When Bev felt herself getting close, Laurie didn't leave it to chance. He took her back to Merrigum, farming the other kids out to relatives and neighbours along the way like parcels that needed safe keeping. It was practical. It was deliberate.

The bus had long since been replaced by a two-tone EH station wagon, towing the old camp wagon behind it. The shafts had been removed years before and replaced with a welded steel drawbar — the same bones as always, just dragged forward now by something with an engine instead of a heartbeat.

Laurie had hired a couple of stock hands and even a temporary cook to manage the cattle they were moving down towards Newmarket. He was learning, slowly, that not everything had to be carried on his own back.

When the pains settled into something steady, Bev didn't wait for anyone.

Her father had long since stopped driving, but the old Dodge still sat in the shed, dust-coated and faithful. She started it herself and pointed it towards Kyabram, eleven miles of bitumen and back road between her and the hospital.

She made it with fifteen minutes to spare.

The nurses were astonished at the size of the baby she delivered — ten pounds, four ounces of solid, determined child. For someone who had barely crossed the threshold in time, she'd done remarkably well.

Years later, when the old Kyabram hospital was turned into the RSL, Timmy would laugh at the thought that he could buy a beer in the same room where he'd first drawn breath.

Bev didn't linger.

The next day she bundled the baby up, signed what needed signing, and drove herself home.

There were no phone calls.

No announcements.

Just the Bush Telegraph.

A word at the yards.

A mention at the pub.

A mail driver passing it on.

By the time it reached Laurie, miles away with his mob, he already knew.

But this time was different.

This time he wasn't putting her back on the road.

He'd already arranged to rent a small semi-detached house in Kyabram.

They didn't stay long — just long enough for it to feel almost normal.

Long enough for Kim to stay at the same school for more than a term.

Long enough to make proper friends.

Long enough, even, for a birthday party.

It wasn't elaborate. Fairy bread. Sausage rolls. A cake Bev iced herself, slightly lopsided but heavy on sprinkles. The EH sat out front with the camp wagon hitched behind it like a reminder that this was only borrowed ground.

The house felt full in a different way. Not with stockmen's boots or dogs under the table, but with children's voices bouncing off plaster walls.

Timmy was only weeks old. Solid from the start.

Bev had just settled him when Kim burst in mid-sentence.

"Mum, can we—"

She stopped.

Timing has never been Bev's strong suit when it comes to spectacle.

As Timmy latched, the let-down caught her unawares and a sharp arc of milk shot clean across the room, catching the light before splashing harmlessly against the far wall.

Kim froze.

Then she did what only a seven-year-old can do.

"Quick! Quick! Come look at this!"

Feet thundered down the hallway.

Children skidded into the doorway.

Some shrieked with laughter.

Others stood open-mouthed in shock.

Two bolted straight back outside like they'd witnessed something forbidden.

Bev, mortified, shifted Timmy under her blouse.

"Out. All of you."

The room emptied in a rush of giggles and scandalised whispers.

Outside, the commentary continued.

"Did you see that?"

"It went across the room!"

"My Mum doesn't do that!"

Kim lingered a second too long.

"Kim," Bev said quietly.

She vanished.

Bev looked down at Timmy, entirely unconcerned with the drama he'd caused.

Out on the long paddock, modesty had never been practical. Babies were fed where they needed feeding. Privacy was measured in minutes, not walls.

But in a semi-detached house with lace curtains and birthday guests, it felt suddenly different.

Later, after the cake crumbs were swept up and the house quietened, Bev found herself laughing — not loudly, just that private laugh that comes when dignity slips sideways.

# CHAPTER EIGHT - Keeping the Camp Fed

By the time Timmy was old enough to remember the camps, droving life had settled into its own rhythm. The dogs knew their work, and whatever they were living out of at the time — wagon, bus, EH station wagon, or whatever was carrying the family down the road — held everything they owned. The children learned quickly how to live off whatever the road provided.

On long droving trips the sheep weren't just cargo — they were the pantry.

Each contract came with an allocation of what drovers called "killers" — sheep they were allowed to butcher along the road for the crew. A typical four-month trip might allow three of them. It didn't sound like much when you said it out loud, but handled properly one sheep could feed a camp for the better part of a week.

Laurie would pick one from the mob in the evening when the sheep had settled and the dogs were curled up under the wagon. The sheep would be taken quietly away from the mob and slaughtered just beyond the light of the fire.

There were rules about it.

When a drover killed a sheep from the mob he was responsible for, he had to prove it had been used for camp meat and not quietly sold off along the road. So Laurie always kept the ear with the brand inside it. That ear stayed with the camp until the next check with the owner or agent, proof that the sheep had been taken honestly for food and nothing else.

It was bush accounting, simple and understood by everyone who worked the long paddock.

After the sheep was killed Laurie salted the carcass down and hung it overnight from a low tree branch. It always had to be hung first. The air cooled the meat and let the juices run clear before it was cut up the next day.

The dogs knew when a killer had been taken.

They would sit just outside the circle of firelight, tails thumping, noses twitching, watching every move Laurie made. That night they ate well — scraps, bones, whatever trimmings came off first. A good dog earned his share.

By morning the carcass would be cut down and divided. The meat was kept in a large drum with a light brine made from salt and the juices that had dripped from the hanging carcass. It wasn't refrigeration, but it was enough to keep the meat sound while they worked their way through it.

Bev had her own quiet system for using every part.

The first night usually meant roast shoulder in the camp oven. The camp oven sat in the coals beside the fire, a heavy cast-iron pot with a lid strong enough to hold shovels of glowing embers. Heat came from above and below, turning it into a bush oven. The shoulder would sit there for hours, slow-cooking while the mob settled and the dogs dozed in the dust.

By the time the lid came off, the meat was falling apart and the smell drifted across the camp like a promise kept.

The next night might be chops, kept cool in the little kerosene fridge that rode in the wagon. Bev would fry them quickly in a pan over the fire while the billy boiled for tea.

After that came the tougher cuts.

Stew from the neck and scrag, bubbling slowly in the camp oven with onions and whatever vegetables they'd managed to pick up in the last town. Tough meat softened with time and heat, turning into thick, rich gravy that soaked straight into damper.

Later in the week came soup, made from shanks and bones boiled down into a broth strong enough to stand a spoon upright. Nothing was wasted. The last of the bones would simmer for hours while the fire burned low.

By the end of it all, a single sheep had fed the camp night after night in a quiet rotation of meals — roast, chops, stew, soup — until there was little left but clean bones and satisfied dogs.

Sometimes the road offered small luxuries.

If they passed another drover pushing cattle the conversation often turned to food.

A bit of lamb might be swapped for a bit of beef, just for the change of it. Drovers understood that after days of the same meat even a small variation could feel like a feast.

And every so often the postman would come rattling along the stock route, bringing mail, bread, or a small parcel from the agent. He might stop for a yarn and a cup of tea while the billy boiled, leaning against the wagon wheel while the sheep breathed softly in the dust behind them.

Out there on the long paddock, meals weren't fancy, but they carried their own quiet importance.

After a day of dust, dogs, and sheep stretching to the horizon, the campfire, the smell of meat in the camp oven, and the clink of tin plates was enough to make the empty country feel almost like home.

Most of the time the killers lasted well enough if they were managed carefully. Bev stretched every sheep the way she stretched everything else in that life — quietly, methodically, without fuss

But the road didn't always respect neat planning.

Some stretches of country were longer than expected. Work slowed. Supplies ran thin. And sometimes the killers ran low before the next town or the next payment.

When that happened, Laurie made sure the dogs were fed first.

A drover could skip a meal if he had to, but a working dog could not. Without the dogs the mob scattered and the job was finished before it began.

So if meat for the camp was running short, Laurie might ride out with the rifle and bring back a kangaroo. The meat wasn't much good for people unless you were desperate, but the dogs thrived on it. Bev would cut it into rough chunks and boil it down in the camp pot until the smell drifted across the reserve and twenty-two dogs sat in a neat half circle waiting their turn.

But kangaroo didn't always stretch far enough either.

On a few long runs, when the killers had nearly been used up and the next town still lay days away, Laurie had another quiet arrangement with one of the dogs.

That dog was Tiger.

Tiger was one of the day dogs, steady and quiet on the mob, but every now and then he had another job to do. It tended to happen more on cattle work, when there were little or no killers allotted and fresh meat was harder to come by. When supplies ran low and they'd been living off what little they could carry, Laurie would send him through the wire fence that marked the edge of the stock reserve and into the cocky's paddock beyond.

He'd crouch low, give a quiet word.

"Go on, Tiger… round 'em up."

Tiger would slip through the wire like smoke.

No bark. No rush. Just gone.

Somewhere out in the darkness he'd find the farmer's mob and begin working them the same way he worked Laurie's sheep — quiet pressure, steady movement, nothing that would startle the whole paddock. A few sheep would drift away from the main mob, not enough to alarm anything, just enough.

Laurie would be waiting at the fence.

Tiger would ease the small group back towards him and Laurie would quietly take one sheep out. Then a soft word, a hand signal, and Tiger would turn the rest back again, guiding them across the paddock until they melted back into the farmer's mob.

By morning everything looked exactly as it had the day before.

In a flock of hundreds, one sheep missing was nothing anyone would ever notice.

Tiger would trot back into camp, calm as you please, curl up near the wagon, and sleep like he'd worked the mob all day.

It wasn't something Laurie relied on often, and he never spoke about it. Just one of those quiet bush arrangements that lived somewhere between necessity and survival.

Back at the fire, Bev would already have the camp oven warming in the coals.

And by morning there would be fresh meat again, the dogs fed, the camp moving, and the long road carrying them on.

But even when meat was scarce, Bev always made sure a little of it was put aside.

Not the best pieces — never those. Just a few rough chunks cut from whatever was left over. She'd leave them sitting in a small tin or hanging in the shade of the wagon where the heat of the day would begin to turn them. After a day or two the smell would sharpen and the edges would darken.

That was exactly how she wanted it.

Because whenever they camped near a farmer's dam or waterhole, the kids knew what was coming next.

Bev would cut the meat into square chunks and hand them out with lengths of string, each about five metres long. The children would tie one end tight around the meat and hold the other like a small fishing line.

Standing on the muddy edge of the dam, they'd swing the meat around their heads a few times like a sling and then fling it out into the water.

The free end of the string was tied to a small stick pushed into the mud at the edge of the bank.

Then everyone waited.

Sometimes nothing happened for a while. The water would sit still, dragonflies skimming across the surface, the mob grazing somewhere behind them.

But every now and then the stick would move — just the slightest fraction.

That was the sign.

The kids would creep forward and begin slowly pulling the string in, hand over hand, gentle as you please. Somewhere under the surface a yabby would be clamped onto the meat with stubborn determination, refusing to let go.

Gradually the top of its shell would begin to show above the water.

Two claws.

A pair of feelers.

Then with a quick hard yank the yabby would come sailing out of the water and land on the bank still clamped stubbornly onto the meat like it owned it.

The kids would scramble after it before it could make a dash back for the water, grabbing it carefully behind the big front claws so it couldn't swing those pincers back onto their fingers. The bigger buggers could easily draw blood if you weren't paying attention.

Once caught, the tail would be flipped up under its belly.

A quick check underneath told the story.

If there were little black dots clustered under the belly or tail, it meant the yabby was a female carrying eggs.

Back into the dam she went.

Females and little ones were always sent back to grow.

The rest went into the bucket with the others, claws rattling against the tin as they piled up.

Later that night Bev would tip them into a pot of boiling water over the fire. The shells turned bright red in the steam while the kids waited nearby with tin plates ready.

After days of lamb — roast lamb, stew lamb, soup lamb — yabbies felt like a feast.

Out on the long paddock, a change of flavour was sometimes all it took to lift a whole camp's spirits.

For the children it was just another small adventure beside a stock reserve. For Bev it was simply the work of keeping the camp fed and the road moving. At the time it all felt ordinary, but the long paddock wasn't going to stay the same forever.

Droving work began to thin. Fences multiplied. Trucks replaced stock routes.

They took more station jobs. More shearing contracts.

Laurie would go ahead as a station hand, sometimes staying on long enough to take a mob back on the road. Bev would remain behind, cooking for shearers and jackeroos, feeding men who worked like they were paid by the mouthful.

She'd wait for word.

A message passed through someone.

A truck driver mentioning Laurie was on his way back.

Sometimes, though, waiting didn't suit.

If school broke for holidays, or the weather held fine over a long weekend, Bev would load the kids into the EH, hitch up what needed hitching, and head towards the last place Laurie had been seen.

There was rarely an exact location.

Just a direction.

"Headed north."

"Camped near the old timber bridge."

"Should be a day or two past Mitiamo."

That was enough.

Once they reached the last known point, the rest was simple.

You didn't need signposts.

You followed the cattle.

Fresh dung in the dust told you how long ago they'd passed. Flattened grass showed where the mob had drifted off the road. A broken fence wire, a scuffed gate, a swirl of hoofprints at a creek crossing — the land carried its own instructions.

The kids learned to spot it before they could properly spell.

"There!" one would call. "They went this way."

And Bev would ease the wagon forward, reading the ground as naturally as she once read a recipe.

By dusk, more often than not, they'd crest a rise and see camp smoke lifting in the distance.

Laurie would look up from the fire as if he'd been expecting them all along.

He never showed surprise.

Just that small lift of the chin. A half-smile under the brim of his hat. As though wives and children emerging from the dusk were the most ordinary thing in the world.

The kids would scatter first — straight to the dogs, to the bedrolls, to whatever pot was simmering on the coals. There was always noise when they arrived. Laughter. Questions. A quick accounting of who had grown, who had learned something new, who had lost a tooth.

Bev would step down last.

Not dramatic. Not sentimental.

Just there.

And by morning, they would be part of the movement again.

That was the rhythm.

Find him.

Fall in beside him.

Move with him.

Until it was time to break away again.

Sometimes they stayed only a night or two. Sometimes longer, if school allowed it and the road was gentle. The children learned to rise with the camp, to roll swags, to carry tin mugs without spilling. They knew how to read the cattle almost as well as they read each other.

But repetition has weight.

When Fiona arrived, the pattern barely shifted on the surface. Five children now. Five sets of shoes by the door. Five voices layered over one another in the back of the EH. The wagon still trailed behind like a stubborn memory of horse days.

Chasing Laurie didn't get easier with more children. It just got louder.

On one of those trips, Bev had gone ahead to make camp, pushing on so the fire would be going and the billy hot by the time the mob came through. Timmy and Fiona had stayed back with Laurie. It made sense at the time. They were only a couple of miles behind.

But Fiona was tired. Overtired. The kind that folds in on itself and then explodes. Timmy wasn't much better.

Laurie did what bush people did then. He waved down the first passing car.

It was an elderly couple, neat and careful, heading through without hurry. Laurie leaned in at the window and explained — wife up the road, just a mile or two ahead, could they drop the little ones off as they passed.

They didn't hesitate.

Timmy and Fiona were lifted into the back seat like parcels being transferred between stations. The old couple even handed them a paper bag of grapes to keep them quiet.

By the time Bev saw the car crest the rise towards camp, she was already walking out to meet it.

Today, you wouldn't risk it. Not for a moment. They could have been halfway to Adelaide before anyone realised what had happened.

But back then, trust travelled the same roads as cattle. You relied on the kindness of strangers because most of the time, they weren't strangers at all. Just people passing through the same country.

It sounds reckless now. It probably was. But from the outside, it all looked like adventure.

There was even a story done up in the Australasian Post — "Daddy's Gone a Droving… and Taken the Kids."

It made for a good headline with a photograph of nappies strung from the wagon on a jimmy-rigged clothesline, the One Tree Plain stretching flat and endless behind them.

But photographs never show the packing.

They don't show the quiet tears when a friend isn't there next term. They don't show the arithmetic of school reports arriving late, or the way Bev would sit at a borrowed table helping with sums by lantern light after cooking for a shed full of shearers.

They don't show the tiredness.

75

As fencing replaced long stock routes and trucks began swallowing distances that once took weeks, droving changed. Work came in patches. Contracts shortened. Station jobs filled the gaps.

Laurie would go ahead more often now.

He'd take a position as a station hand, or stay long enough to move a herd through. Bev would remain behind with the children, cooking in shearing sheds, renting small houses when she could, building temporary normality wherever they landed.

She still followed sometimes.

But less.

School began to matter more than romance.

Friendships that lasted longer than a season.

And slowly, without any formal decision, Bev stayed put more often when Laurie took the road.

Not because she loved the life any less.

Not because she feared it.

But because five children needed something steadier than horizons.

The long paddock had shaped them.

It had taught them resilience, adaptability, loyalty.

But it would not raise them forever.

And for the first time, the road did not feel like the only direction forward.

# CHAPTER NINE - The Bush, the School Run, and the Woman Who Did It All

There was nothing sparse about Triple J Ranch now. It clung to the slope just below Mount Beauty, tucked into the folds of the Kiewa Valley where the hills rose steep and green against the spine of the Victorian Alps. The bush here was thick and lush — mountain ash and messmate towering overhead, wattles crowding the gullies, tree ferns unfurling in the damp shade. In the mornings, mist pooled low and silver between the trunks, and the air smelt of wet leaf litter and river stone.

It was a different world from the one-tree plains of central Victoria, where paddocks ran flat and exposed to the horizon and wind pushed unbroken across dry grass and fence lines. Out there, properties sat wide and sun-bleached under a hard sky, separated by miles of wire and dust. Here, land folded in on itself. Fences bent with the contours. You didn't look out across distance — you looked up into canopy.

There were still no shops within walking distance, no casual drop-ins over a boundary fence, but the isolation felt different. Not the stark loneliness of open plains, but a green, enclosing quiet. Birds called from every layer of the forest — currawongs, rosellas, the distant laugh of kookaburras — and after rain you could hear the Kiewa River moving somewhere below the slope.

Two hundred metres of cleared earth circled the house like a defensive moat — scraped back to dirt and short grass, woodpiles stacked well away from the walls, gutters kept clean and ready. Beyond that line, though, the bush rose abruptly and unapologetic, undergrowth thick and damp, tree ferns massed in the gullies. It didn't press against the verandah rails, but it waited just beyond the clearing, dense and watchful, as if it would reclaim the space the moment they let it.

Bev stood at the edge of the verandah, staring down the narrow gravel track that twisted its way towards the Carboor schoolhouse. Beyond that, there was nothing but bush. It wasn't a straight dirt line carved across flat country. It dipped and climbed, curved around gullies, disappeared behind stands of timber so dense they seemed to swallow sound. In central Victoria, you could see weather coming for miles. Here, it arrived without warning — fog rolling in, storms spilling over the ranges.

The track was still the only way in or out. But instead of cutting through emptiness, it tunneled through green shadow. And today, like most days, it was calling her — not across open plains, but into the folds of the mountain.

The Hill

The storm had rolled down off the ranges two nights earlier without warning. Not a polite mountain shower, but a hard, sideways thing — wind snapping branches, rain hammering tin, the kind that rattled windows and left the bush rearranged by morning.

In the Kiewa Valley, storms didn't just pass through. They dropped limbs across tracks, loosened red clay, and turned slopes into skating rinks.

She had five kids now. Four needed to get to the one-room school at Carboor, just a 25 minute drive, if the track behaved,  which it rarely did. The youngest wasn't yet two, and she wasn't the kind of child who could be left behind.

Bev packed her into the old station wagon along with her siblings then hoisted the chainsaw into the back.

You didn't go anywhere in the bush without tools. Not if you wanted to get there, especially after a storm like this one..

The kids clambered in, squabbling over damp raincoats and trying not to sit on each other's sandwiches. There were no seatbelts, of course. No fancy child seats. Fiona wobbled between the front seats like a sailor in high seas, gripping the headrest with one chubby hand and clutching a crust of bread with the other.

Bev turned the key. The engine coughed awake.

They bumped down the track, stopping twice to clear fallen limbs — Bev cursing under her breath as she sawed through trunks and rolled them aside with aching arms. The storm two nights ago had taken its toll. Every mile demanded something.

And then they reached *the Hill.*

It loomed ahead, steep and slick, a near 45-degree climb over 250 metres of red, rain-soaked clay. Bev didn't hesitate. She slammed the gear into first, gritted her teeth, and gunned it.

You could hear the grit scatter under the wheels, the occasional slap of water being thrown from the tyres, and the metallic rasp of effort in the engine's tone, like it's wrestling the road itself. As the car inches upward, the engine's voice becomes almost desperate, flickering between hope and struggle, louder and more labored with each second.

The car shudders, then pauses, its tyres spinning for a moment longer in place, spitting up mud and gravel — before it begins to slide backward. Slowly at first, almost hesitantly, like a beast losing its footing, it surrenders to the slope. The engine's growl turns to a frustrated sputter, throttled but helpless.

As the wheels roll in reverse, the car tilts slightly, sliding unevenly over the rutted, rain-slick dirt track. The wet earth squelches and gives way, and the tyres cut deep gouges as they fail to grip, skimming over loose stones and patches of slick clay.

Inside, Bev feels a slow tilting drop in your stomach. Outside, there's the unmistakable grinding crunch of undercarriage against rising ridges of dirt. A thud here, a lurch there, the vehicle jerks unpredictably, caught between gravity and terrain. The brakes squeal as she fights for control, but the hill pulls it down, indifferent.

Bev grips the wheel tight, jaw clenched, eyes fixed on the slick incline ahead. She shifts into reverse, letting the car roll back down the track until there's just enough space — maybe twenty feet — not much, but enough for a run-up. The rain taps steadily on the roof, a quiet warning she chooses to ignore.

She breathes in once. Hard. Then slams the gear into first.

The engine snarls back to life, and she floors it, mud spraying behind as the tyres dig in and the car lunges forward, bouncing slightly on the uneven track. For a moment, the wheels grip, and she surges up the incline. But halfway there, traction slips. The engine screams, wheels spinning faster than they're moving, and the car lurches sideways, tyres losing the fight against the slick clay. It skids, falters, and slides backward again.

Undeterred, Bev tries again. And again.

Each time, she backs up just far enough, revs the engine, and charges forward, teeth gritted like she's trying to will the car up by force alone. Mud flies. The scent of burning clutch lingers. The wheels bite for seconds and then betray her, slipping with a sickening jolt that sends the car drifting sideways, inches from a shallow ditch.

Behind her, the back seat is a jumble of raincoats, school bags, and restless limbs — four kids, aged 6 to 12, and a toddler, who stands wobbling between the front seats, clutching the headrest like it's the mast of a ship in a storm. No seat belts. No straps. Just a mess of kids trying to stay upright while their mother wrestles the car and the hill.

The toddler's been fussing for the last ten minutes, face red and damp with frustration. The older kids bounce with every bump, caught somewhere between mild panic and Monday-morning boredom.

"Are we gonna make it this time, Mum?" the eldest asks, eyeing the slope ahead.

Bev doesn't answer. She shifts into reverse, rolling the car back down the rutted track until there's enough space. Not much, but it'll have to do. She takes a breath, tightens her grip, then slams the car into first.

The engine growls, tyres kick up mud and stones, and the car lunges forward, jerking the kids back in their seats. The toddler shrieks in delight or fear, it's not clear which, as she grabs at Bev's shoulder for balance. For a moment, the wheels grip. The car surges forward, up the incline.

Then traction vanishes.

The tyres whine and spin, the whole car shudders, and they begin to slide back, crooked and slow, like something wounded giving up the fight.

"Hold on!" Bev snaps, one hand steadying the toddler, the other wrestling the wheel.

The middle child yells, "We're going backward again!"

"I'm gonna be late!" the younger protests, holding his sandwich bag like it's an emergency supply.

Bev swears under her breath and tries again. Reverse. First gear. Another run-up. The car thunders forward, mud spraying the sides, the kids bouncing like laundry in a tumble dryer. But the result is the same — half up, then skidding back down, the engine roaring in protest.

After another failed run, the toddler is crying, arms raised towards Bev, wanting to be held. The older kids have gone quiet, clinging to door handles and each other. The rain sheets down harder now, and the track has turned to a mess of slippery clay and sharp-edged stones.

One last try. She floors it.

The car slips almost immediately, rear wheels fishtailing before the whole vehicle slides sideways, down into a muddy hollow that sucks at the tyres like it means to swallow them whole.

The engine chokes, then dies.

Silence settles, broken only by the sound of rain on the roof, the tick of cooling metal, and the soft sniffles of a muddy, barefoot toddler now crawling into Bev's lap.

She leans her head back against the seat, staring up at the sagging roof liner, breathing hard.

The hill has won. And school will have to wait.

Then a small voice piped up from the back seat.

"But... Mum," someone stammered, eyes wide, "how are we gonna get home?"

Bev sighed, wiping her hands on her jeans. She muttered something under her breath and gave the steering wheel a thump. The road behind was churned into a mess, and the road ahead was a greasy clay slope that laughed in the face of almost any vehicle.

Everyone looked at Bev. Even the dog looked worried.

Then, without a second thought, Kim, the oldest at just 12 chimed "I'll go get help."

There was a beat of silence, half surprise, half disbelief, but Kim was already grabbing the water bottle and pulling on her boots like it was the most normal thing in the world. She knew the country, knew the track, and she knew the rough direction to the next property having walked it many times before just to visit a friend.

Bev hesitated. "You sure, love?"

Kim nodded. "It's only a few miles if I cut through the scrub. I'll be quicker than sitting here waiting for someone to come by."

With that, she set off. No fuss, no drama, just a long-legged stride into the bush, dodging puddles and ducking under branches as the wagon slowly disappeared behind her.

Time passed slowly. The little ones squabbled, someone cried, someone else fell asleep. Bev kept glancing at the horizon, chewing the inside of her cheek.

Then, finally, hours later, a distant engine growled in the still air.

Over the ridge came a lumbering, mud-splattered tractor, chugging along like it had all the time in the world. And there, perched proudly on the side step in a spray of red mud, was Kim, grinning ear to ear, looking like she'd just conquered a mountain.

With a lurch and a roar, the station wagon was dragged out of the worst of it, and back onto solid ground.

Bev gave Kim a hug that nearly knocked her boots off, and promised she could ride up front for the trip home, no arguments.

From then on, whenever the road got tough or the map got fuzzy, someone would always say with a grin:

"Well, if all else fails… we'll just send Kim."

Fire in the Bush

The Australian bush is a world of ever-shifting moods, a place where seasons don't so much change as they transform, sometimes slowly, sometimes with barely a warning. Summer could settle in like a heavy cloak, the days stretching long and hot, the air dry enough to crack timber and split the earth. Then without warning, a storm could roll in from the south, the sky darkening to bruise-black, thunder rumbling low like some old beast waking. In winter, mist hung low in the valleys like a second ground, and the nights could drop cold enough to frost the grass stiff, even as the midday sun burned it away by lunch. The bush never stayed still, it breathed, it shifted, and it watched.

One year, the dry came early, and it stayed. The creeks shrank to a trickle. The grass grew brittle. The air grew tense.

And then the bushfire came.

It started a long way off, just smoke on the horizon. But in the bush, distances lie. Smoke means trouble. It moves fast.

Like all able-bodied men in the district, Laurie went off to help, riding out with the local fire crew to dig breaks and backburn, a volunteer with nothing but a water pack, a shovel, and grim determination. Fires out here weren't tame or tactical, they were wild, unpredictable things that leapt ridges and changed direction with the wind, sometimes skipping entire valleys, then doubling back like they'd forgotten something.

While Laurie was gone, the fire turned.

The wind picked up, fierce and erratic, and the blaze wrapped around Tripple J Ranch, cutting off the only road in and out. The property was surrounded, a red, churning wall of heat just beyond the trees.

Bev and the kids were on their own.

She didn't hesitate. She filled every drum, bucket, and tin she could find with water. The kids, still young, but already toughened by bush life, fell into line without question. Rags were soaked and kept handy. Old sacks were laid on the verandah, wet and ready to beat down sparks. The air was thick with smoke, stinging the eyes and throat. The toddler clung to Bev's leg while she moved from one side of the house to the other, eyes scanning the glowing sky, listening for the crackle of embers landing on the tin roof or in the dry garden.

Every so often, one of the kids would yell "Mum! Over here!", and they'd run with sloshing buckets to douse a small flame starting in the grass, or beat out smoldering leaves with wet towels.

The fire never fully breached the cleared land, but the embers rained down like burning snow, and each one was a threat.

They worked like that, tired, frightened, but focused, for nearly two days, sleeping in shifts, barely eating, ears tuned to the wind, eyes on the trees.

When Laurie finally made it back, smoke-blackened, exhausted, eyes rimmed red, he found the homestead still standing, the house untouched, the kids asleep in a line on the verandah, Bev sitting upright in a chair, bucket still at her feet, watching the tree line.

She looked up at him, weary but steady.

"It came close," she said simply.

And Laurie just nodded, too choked up to speak.

In the bush, you learned quickly that survival wasn't just about strength, it was about knowing the land, respecting it, and having the grit to stand your ground when everything told you to run.

Tripple J Ranch survived that fire,  not because it got lucky, but because Bev and the kids fought for it, ember by ember, bucket by bucket, breath by breath.

The Great Pig Escape

It was supposed to be an ordinary morning, feed the chooks, boil the billy, sort out the kids, and get a few loads of washing done before the heat set in. But nothing at Tripple J Ranch ever stayed ordinary for long.

Bev was halfway through hanging a line of shirts when she noticed the baby piglet, a curious little pink escape artist, trotting confidently across the paddock, tail twitching like it owned the place.

"Hey! Get back here, you little bugger!" she shouted, dropping the peg basket and lifting her apron.

The piglet squealed and darted, legs skittering as it made for the open paddock, nose up, ears flapping with each bounce. Bev gave chase without a second thought, her outdoor slippers slapping softly as she ran, determined despite their thin soles.

The kids, watching from the verandah, paused mid-mouthful of Weet-Bix. This was better than television.

The piglet zigzagged between tussocks of grass, around the old dog kennel, and straight towards the blackberry bush that marked the far edge of the clearing. Bev was right behind it, dodging divots, breath coming in short bursts, laughing in spite of herself.

"You're not faster than me, mate!"

She lunged forward, arms outstretched, and that's when the world tilted.

Her foot slipped. The grass gave way. And Bev, drover's wife, bush cook, fire-beater, and mother of five, let out a high-pitched squeal of her own as she tumbled backward into the blackberry bush, arms flailing like a windmill gone rogue.

She landed with a rustle, a thump, and a gasp.

The piglet stopped short, turned, gave her a brief sniff, and wandered off, unimpressed.

From the paddock, Bev's voice rang out:

Someone! Get me out of this bloody bush porcupine!"

The blackberry thorns had claimed her completely. One slipper was already gone. The other hung off her heel. Her arms were tangled in vines, her apron caught, and her pride thoroughly pricked.

The kids were doubled over with laughter now.

Vicki shouted from the gate, "Mum! You alright?"

"Do I look alright?" she snapped, trying to lift her backside out of the tangle without losing the other slipper. "I'm tangled up like the Sunday roast in butcher's string!"

Eventually, the older kids got to her, trying very hard not to smile as they looked down at Mum, flat on her back, stuck in a blackberry bush one barefoot and scratches blooming red on her arms.

"Just help me out before I become the next bloody scarecrow!"

It took some effort, a lot of swearing, and a broken twig in someone's ear, but they finally got her free, limping, scratched, half shoeless, but triumphant in spirit.

The piglet, by then, had found its way back to the pen and was napping peacefully in the shade.

Timmy and The Great Bike Ride

It was one of those classic outback afternoons, dry, dusty, and full of chaos. Bev, Laurie, and the five kids had packed into the station wagon and bounced their way over to a neighbouring ranch to visit friends. It wasn't long before the grown-ups had settled in with tea and gossip, while the kids scattered like wild goats across the yard.

Between both families, there were about ten kids running riot, and only one pushbike.

Now, this wasn't just any pushbike. It was a battered old thing with one working brake and faded red paint, but to the kids, it was gold. Treasure. Freedom on wheels. And naturally, everyone wanted a turn.

But patience was in short supply, and after several screaming matches, two full-blown wrestling bouts, and a dramatic accusation of "he's had it for ten minutes!", the adults had had enough. Laurie, with a huff, hoisted the bike up and dumped it on the roof of the tin shed.

Out of sight, out of mind? Hardly.

The bike sat there, like a glittering prize. And it wasn't long before Timmy, seven years old and apparently born without fear, decided he wasn't about to let a bit of tin roofing come between him and his destiny.

He climbed the shed like a feral cat, scrambled up the side, and somehow managed to wrangle the bike upright. But as he pushed it towards the edge, one wheel jammed in the groove of the corrugated iron roof. Of course, that didn't stop Timmy. Oh no, he rode it. Or rather, he tried to.

Timmy didn't stop pedalling, not even when the front wheel dipped over the edge of the shed roof.

For a half-second, it looked like he might defy gravity altogether, legs still spinning furiously, handlebars gripped tight, determination in every limb. But the air beneath the tyres quickly reminded him he was no magician.

The bike, wedged in the corrugation just a moment earlier, lurched free and tipped forward, carrying Timmy with it. And still, he pedalled. Out of instinct, stubbornness, or sheer panic, no one really knows. But those feet kept going, round and round, even as he and the bike launched into thin air like a badly-planned circus stunt.

He went down wheels first, then headfirst, still pedalling all the way into a tangle of barbed wire, dust, and disaster.

It was the most determined descent anyone had ever seen, and somehow, despite landing in a fence, he walked away with only five stitches and a story that no one would ever forget.

The bike stayed on the roof after that, but no one tried to climb up again.

Except maybe once. But that's another story.

Heading to the Big Smoke

Every month or so, Bev would load the kids into the station wagon, leaving Laurie behind on the property, and make the two-hour drive to the big smoke for supplies.

The big smoke was Albury–Wodonga , the twin cities, or so they liked to call themselves,  sitting astride the great Murray River like a place unsure whether it was still a country town or already becoming something else. Albury carried the weight of history and order: wide streets, solid brick buildings, clocks that ran on Sydney time. Wodonga, on the other hand, felt newer and rougher around the edges, shaped by paddocks, factories, and the steady movement of working families. The Murray slid between them, brown and patient, crossed daily by people who barely noticed the border anymore. Life moved at an unhurried pace. Shopfronts closed early, football ruled the weekends, and the river and the dam offered escape from the heat. There was optimism in the air, but also a sense that change was coming, not yet visible, just felt, like a distant train still beyond the horizon.

Bonegilla lay just beyond the towns, half hidden among paddocks and red dust, close to the broad stillness of the Hume Dam, a place spoken about as much as it was seen. Rows of weathered huts stretched across the old army ground, their tin roofs catching the same sun that glinted off the lake nearby. Each one held stories carried from elsewhere: voices thick with unfamiliar languages, memories of cities left behind, and hopes sharpened by necessity. At night, light spilled from small windows and mingled with the sound of radios, laughter, arguments, and songs that did not belong to Australia yet were already changing it.

For Albury and Wodonga, Bonegilla was both close and distant, like the dam itself, ever present, yet easily overlooked. Locals passed the camp's gates on the road to the water and saw people milling inside, walking between huts, hanging washing, talking in clusters that sounded nothing like home. To them it was a place of "new Australians," a steady source of labour for farms, factories, and building sites. Men arrived at worksites with strong backs and quiet determination; women appeared in shops and schools, learning the rhythms of a new country while holding onto the old. Accents softened over time, names were shortened, and unfamiliar foods slowly found their way into kitchens and cafés, reshaping the towns almost without notice.

Bonegilla carried a heavier meaning too, shaped by the same post-war ambition that had raised the dam and promised security and growth. It was one of the country's first real encounters with mass migration, proof that Australia was no longer just Anglo and inward-looking, but something broader, louder, and more complicated. The camp was a threshold: harsh, temporary, and often lonely, set beside a vast man-made lake that spoke of permanence and control. And as they drove past those gates, dust rising and the camp alive with movement, little Timmy could never have imagined that somewhere among the faces passing by was a small, blonde Nordic girl from the opposite side of the world , carrying her own memories and hopes, who would one day step into his life and quietly steal his heart.

The cinema sat just around the corner from the SSW supermarket. Bev would drop the four older kids off at the pictures and take the youngest with her to do the shopping. The little one was still too young to even know what a movie was. She usually timed it just right, finishing the groceries as the cinema doors opened and the kids spilled out, ready for the long drive back to the ranch.

Then came the trip. The special trip. No movies. No cinema. On a school day. And Dad came too.

Everyone had to help with the shopping — everyone except Timmy. He went with Laurie to the local police station instead. Timmy watched as his father filled out paperwork, slid some money across the counter, and received a single piece of paper in return. From there they crossed the street to Harbreicht's Electrical Store, and that's where it happened.

They bought a television.

Not just any television. It was a His Master's Voice three-in-one entertainment unit: a wood-grain, black-and-white valve TV, an AM/SW radio, and a record player that could handle 78s, 45s, and 33s, complete with a record stacker so you could play one after another without lifting a finger.

Back at the ranch, the TV was installed and hooked up to the giant antenna on the roof which Dad convinced the kids was some newfangled weather vane. With the unheard-of treat of a bag of popcorn, they sat down to watch Lassie Come Home. Kim and Vicki huddled together on the couch, crying at every chore and tribulation Lassie endured. Timmy bounced up and down, shouting, "It's okay! Lassie will win!" And Shane, well Shane just sat there, dumbfounded, eyes glued to the idiot box. The popcorn passed him at least ten times without him taking a single kernel.

As night settled over the paddocks and the glow from the television spilled across the walls, something quietly shifted in the house. The outback hadn't let go of them, the dust, the distance, the rhythm of the land were still there, but a door had opened. From a life shaped by isolation and self-reliance, they were stepping, almost without noticing, into a world more connected, more crowded with voices and stories from far beyond the horizon. The screen flickered, the antenna creaked in the wind, and the family sat together on the edge of something new, leaving one way of living behind while not yet knowing what the next would ask of them.

The Day the Little Bush School Closed

For the first time in years, they made a choice that wasn't just about cattle or contracts, they based themselves on a modest ranch near a small bush school, that offered semi-permanent work. The school wasn't much, but it had a classroom, a teacher, and a bell. And that was enough.

The kids flourished in their own wild way, barefoot at recess, ponies after class, helping with yard work before dark. It was rough and ready, but it was home.

But time didn't stop.

When Kim, the eldest, finished Grade 6, there were no more grades left at the little school. It was strictly primary. No high school, no next step.

Bev couldn't bring herself to send Kim off to boarding school in the city. Instead, they agreed she'd go live with Nan and Pop back in Merrigum to start high school. It was practical, but it pulled at Bev like a loose stitch.

The months passed. Kim grew into town routines. And one day, Bev looked at the younger kids and realised they'd all be following soon. That night, leaning against the yard rails, she turned to Laurie and said "we've done the hard yards. It's time to settle somewhere, a proper town, with schools, doctors, shops. Give the kids a better run."

Laurie didn't argue. He gave a quiet nod. That was all.

So they packed up their gear, said goodbye to life on the road, and moved into a small town. It wasn't easy, leaving behind the open space, the work, the freedom, but they knew it was the right thing.

Only, when they left, it hit the community harder than expected.

Their four kids made up almost half the enrolments at the bush school. And without them, there were only six kids left. The education department's rules were clear: a bush school needed at least ten students to stay open.

So it closed.

Just like that. No farewell party. No big announcement. Just an empty classroom and a lonely swing creaking in the wind.

Imagine that... it only took one family to break a school.

# EPILOGUE - When the Road Grew Quiet

In town, life was busier, sports days, traffic, homework spread across a kitchen table that didn't move every few weeks. But the bush never left them. It was in their bones.

Still, life in town brought new adventures. proper footy teams, weekend shops, and friends who lived just down the street instead of forty minutes down a dirt track. And while they missed the wide skies and long silences, the kids thrived.

Over the years that followed, they drifted in and out of town a few more times. Laurie couldn't quite give up the road, he still took the odd mob or herd when the work came calling, and the bush always pulled at him like a well-worn rope. But something had shifted. The kids were growing, school routines had taken root, and the family's days of living full-time on horseback were behind them.

It was the end of an era, not with fanfare or fuss, but in that quiet, unspoken way where life simply turns a page. The kind of change that doesn't make headlines, but stays with you forever.

Bev was the engine of a mobile household, the kind of woman who didn't just hold things together, but made them move. She was the teacher of children, the seamstress, the cook, the gardener, and the quiet protector. She could fish, shoot, sew, skin, salt meat, break a horse, and boil a nappy without missing a beat.

She navigated fires, floods, and backroads that would shake the bolts out of a Land Cruiser. A woman who'd delivered babies between sheep drives, boiled nappies in kerosene tins, and tethered toddlers to wagon shafts just to keep them safe while she worked. She made a home wherever the wheels stopped, raised five kids with one hand on a camp stove and the other steadying the whole world.

When the fire came, she didn't run. When the road failed, she kept driving. That's who she was.

She was the reason they could live the life they did, tough, mobile, raw, and real.

She was never just a wife.